T0208699

An Evangelist's Heart

JANINE Y. ROSS

WESTBOW
PRESS®
A DIVISION OF THOMAS NELSON
& ZONDERVAN

WestBow Press books may be ordered through booksellers or by contacting:

WestBow Press
A Division of Thomas Nelson & Zondervan
1663 Liberty Drive
Bloomington, IN 47403
www.westbowpress.com
1 (866) 928-1240

Scripture taken from the New King James Version®. Copyright ©
1982 by Thomas Nelson. Used by permission. All rights reserved.

ISBN: 978-1-9736-4952-6 (sc)
ISBN: 978-1-9736-4953-3 (hc)
ISBN: 978-1-9736-4951-9 (e)

Library of Congress Control Number: 2018914960

Print information available on the last page.

WestBow Press rev. date: 1/3/2019

Contents

Chapter 1
In the Beginning

M any years ago, when we did what we called *soul winning*, it was commonplace to approach people, introduce yourself and your church's name, and tell them that you wanted to introduce them to Jesus. Hardly anyone would reject our attempts to win his or her soul to Jesus. They would be accommodating, listening intently while we explained the Romans Road to Salvation, which used specific scriptures in the book of Romans to explain the *whats* and the *whys* of people's need for salvation. It was a tract, a small pamphlet that held the written message we were explaining. More times than not, many of those to whom we were witnessing would become so moved by the message of the gospel of Jesus Christ that they would weep, all the while stammering, "Yes, I want to be saved." As this spiritual and emotional window was opening, we would pray with the person the prayer of salvation, thereby ushering that person into a relationship with Jesus Christ, solidifying his or her status as a child of God, newly born into the family of God.

The next step was to invite people to church and help them become acclimated to the life of a Christian. This entailed registering them for discipleship classes. These classes were the equivalent of Christianity 101, because in these classes, "new believers" would receive basic teachings about their new lives in God for the purpose of getting them grounded and stable in this holy lifestyle. These classes ranged from two to sixteen weeks long, and by the end, the new converts would be well versed in what their lives had embarked on, making them ready to begin their journey.

We all started that way. We won souls for the Lord. It was what Jesus meant when He told the disciples in the Bible to "go and compel them to come." And this command was to have a reciprocal effect. One tells another, and that one tells another until the numbers of Christians in the world would outnumber those who were not.

It was easy. Christianity tugged at the heart. It drew people to God. Who could reject the fact that there is a God who loved the world so much that He let His Son die for the sins that they rightfully deserved the punishment for? Who could ignore God's love after realizing He created people for His purposes, that He created them to have abundant life that could only be found in His Son, Jesus? The drawing love of God would woo people back into the original intent He had for them—which had been broken by Adam and Eve at the beginning of time. It is no wonder that the Bible emphasizes in John 15:143, "Greater love has no one than this, than to lay down one's life for his friends." All one had to do was share this knowledge with others and then witness people willingly and almost helplessly render their hearts to God.

But something happened. Something changed. Suddenly, there were other "religions," other beliefs rising up and claiming that their way was the right way, or that Christianity was not the only way. I always felt that some people simply could not stand the fact that God's love was permeating this world so much that droves of people found themselves accepting it as truth.

Consequently, there was the infiltration of strange religions and strange beliefs. People started saying, "Christianity can't be the only way. It can't be the only choice we have." Some would say, "Oh, that doesn't work for me. I need something that suits my needs." What God said in the Bible was no longer relevant. It became, "Whose Bible is that? Who wrote it? I don't want that."

Now we have so many different denominations, beliefs, and religions that, in one way or another, oppose biblical doctrine. Some people felt that one size should not be made to fit all. The Bible as God's one truth made no sense to many, and this led to the birth of the many thousands of alternative ways to believe in God (or not) and the many ways to get to God—if there is a God at all.

Ultimately, Satan, in his angry retaliation against God, conjured up new and untoward religions and has caused such a divide because his one and only agenda is for souls to be lost in hell forever. Hell was made for Satan and his fallen angels. He was thrown out of heaven when he decided to foolishly go against God's authority and attempt to gather a following of his own. He managed to convince some of the angels to align with his wicked agenda, though fruitlessly. They were kicked out of heaven, and from that day until the present time, the war against God and His people has been fierce. Satan knows that his doom is imminent. But to end up in the lake that burns with fire and brimstone all alone, he refuses to accept it. Again, his one and only agenda is to take as many with him as he can. What better way to do that than to deceive the masses into believing that Jesus is not the one and only way to God? Or to deceive them into believing that their need is for some other deity, or to convince people that God doesn't even exist?

Satan has worked his wickedness in many massive yet subtle ways. One woman, Madalyn Murray O'Hair, best known for the 1963 *Murray v. Curlett* lawsuit, pushed her agenda all the way to the Supreme Court, causing Bible reading in schools to be ruled unlawful. A year prior, another high-profile case ultimately prohibited prayer in schools. No longer is any mention of God or Jesus allowed. Though our country was founded on Christian ideals, there is the separation of church and state, which describes a distance between political influence and religious organizations.

Isn't it odd, however, that these very rules and laws are immediately tabled in times of tragedy in our world? During incidences of sadness and grief, the first thing we hear is, "Let us pray." Pray? To whom? This God whose name we are otherwise banned from daring to mention?

How did we end up here?

Where is the Church?

Chapter 2
Where Is the Church?

I took a class at our ministry through an Oral Roberts University certificate program where we learned that there are more than seven hundred or more different religious beliefs. How did we go from Jesus being the only way to having a choice between seven hundred or more religions? I remember talking to a young man at an alternative school where I taught for a short while.

After my whole spiel, he looked at me and said, "Ma'am, it's not that I don't believe you, but everybody says their way is the right way."

I was honestly at a loss for words. As I look back over my life as a witness for the truth of Jesus, I realize that it was the Holy Spirit of God that has taught me how to navigate this mantle called "evangelist." Though I've taken some classes over the years, the truth is, there really is no one way to *train* a person to reach the lost on behalf of Christ. There is no one-size-fits-all approach.

There is no cookie-cutter way to reach people with the gospel of Jesus Christ. We must simply allow the Holy Spirit to lead us in the moment.

I'm often reminded of the scripture in Luke 12:12 that says not to worry about what you will say because the Spirit of God will give you the precise words at the very moment that you need them. When that young man spoke to me, I realized it was not my place to convince him. I had to remind myself that it was the responsibility of the Holy Spirit. I learned that if people's hearts sincerely long for truth, God will make sure His truth finds them. The Lord will make sure to move upon their hearts in such a way that they will have no doubt that Jesus is the only way and that salvation comes by no other, as the Bible reminds us in Acts 4:12. I had only to pray for that young man and believe God would move the scales from his eyes that inhibited his ability to see and receive truth. If I never see him again, I know without a doubt that if he was sincerely seeking truth, God will have revealed it in an undeniable way. It would be left up to that young man, however, to receive it—or not.

In the 1990s I had a friend and coworker who was a Jehovah's Witness. She would listen to our conversations about salvation through Jesus and became inquisitive. She had so many questions, and we tried very hard to answer her in a way that would cause her to want to be saved. The beliefs that the Jehovah's Witnesses had at that time were so ingrained in her that she was torn. But again, it was clear that she longed for truth. She began to go to church with me and was ultimately disowned by her mother. Over the years she struggled, but something about the Christian faith drew her closer and closer. Not long after that, she found out that she had breast cancer, and by the time I found out, she was near death. I remember praying that the Lord would not allow her to leave this world without revealing the truth that I knew she longed for. Bless God that she confided in me that she realized Jesus was the way and had accepted Him as her Savior. As sad as it was that she passed away, my heart rejoiced in knowing that she was with the Lord in heaven.

Again, if a person's heart is sincerely seeking truth, God will make sure the truth finds them. And when it does, their hearts can only become overwhelmed and consumed with the love of God, that it is nearly impossible to deny or reject it. Sadly, though, many do reject God's drawing love. And as God does not interfere with our right to choose, He will step aside and allow someone to whom He has revealed His truth to turn away from so great a love, ultimately choosing their eternity in hell, forever separated from God.

In May 2018 I heard on a television broadcast that seventy thousand people die every day without Jesus. Seventy thousand people per day die and go to eternal torment. But many say, "Oh, but a wonderful, loving God would never 'send' someone to hell." Well, have you ever considered that a wonderful, loving God doesn't "send" people to heaven either? Remember, God will not interfere with our free will. He allows us to choose. Whatever the reasons may be that many reject salvation through Jesus, the truth remains that it is still a choice. It matters not whether they believe it or not, because the Bible says in Deuteronomy 30:18 that God sets before us life and death and He commands us to "choose." He even suggests we choose life, but, again, He will not interfere with our right to choose.

Hell, for so many, even born-again Christians, is a concept that is very hard to accept or believe. To be honest, I admit that there had been times when even I questioned God about the severity of "the lake that burns with fire and brimstone."

The thought of such an end is more than our finite minds can absorb. It's too overwhelming to think of. We tell people they will spend eternity in hell, yet even that is not the be-all and end-all. The Bible tells us in Revelation 20:14 that "death and hell" will be cast into the lake that burns with fire and brimstone for all eternity.

I heard it explained this way when I went to an evangelism conference in March 2018: "If I slap the person next to me, that person can simply slap me back.

If I slap a police officer, that police officer can arrest me. If I slap the king of a country, I can potentially be beheaded. We've all heard the old saying that 'the punishment fits the crime.'"

Well, notice that in the above scenarios, the crime was all the same; however, the punishment was increasingly more severe. Why? Because the punishment must fit the *level of authority* that you offend.

So when people reject God's salvation, that is essentially "slapping God in the face." And what higher authority is there than God? So, the punishment fitting the level of authority offended, those rejecting salvation through Jesus Christ have (figuratively) slapped God (the ultimate authority) in the face. And again, the punishment must match the authority offended. That punishment is what is termed ECT, or eternal conscious torment. Wow! Enough said.

Where is the Church?

In a nutshell, the Church, those who are supposed to represent the truth of God's Word, have, over the years, tucked their tails and run. The Church, the body of Christ, has become the proverbial ostrich that hides its head in a hole in the ground. According to National Geographic, however, ostriches don't really hide their heads in the sand. They dig holes to be used as nests. Several times a day, they reach their heads in the holes and turn their eggs.

In a sense, the Church has dug holes of compromise based on fear and intimidation. They've dug these holes in the name of keeping the peace and being inclusive of all other beliefs, religious or not. The Church is now forced to reach its head in the hole its dug and turn away everything that stands for God's truth. It has been so busy with its head in the hole turning over everything that is the One way, truth, and life that the enemy has come in and sown seeds that have taken root, and now anything goes. The Church has been so busy trying not to offend, trying not to rock the boat, trying not to seem disagreeable on issues of equality, trying not to seem so fanatical, that our world has been inundated with hundreds and thousands of ways to serve God or gods.

The Church has stood back in the shadows; it has attempted to blend in with the crowd, afraid to stand for what God says in His Word. Consequently, Satan has had free reign to deceive the nations. And get this: Satan doesn't have to lift a finger. He just sits back and watches us combat and destroy each other. How? Through competition and territorialism; through allowing us to give our own interpretation of God's Word, though all of us say that we believe the same God and the same Word of God. Satan sits back and watches us make ministry into big business. For many, it is no longer about pointing people to Jesus and the purpose He has for their lives. It has become about who has the most members. It has become about trying to get on TV. It has become about status and position and popularity. Satan has given us the rope and we are hanging ourselves. And in the meantime, the kingdom of darkness has infiltrated our world in such a way that it almost seems hopeless to try to lead people back to God's original intent. God wants to save souls and reveal His purpose for our lives; He wants to give us abundant life and ultimately usher us into the best part of all, when this life is over, eternity in heaven with Him.

Division among churches is at an epidemic proportion. There is a church on almost every corner, on almost every block in some places, yet there is no collaboration; there is no sharing or working toward God's one common goal, which is to seek and save the lost. There is so much jealousy, envy, control, and territorialism among the churches that some would rather have five members than to join with others of like mind and faith to accomplish the mission of God. How are we missing the fact that seventy thousand people die—unsaved—every day? Could some have been people we passed by from time to time and never said a word to? Could they have been family members or friends?

Where is the Church?

While the Church has lost its way, the Bible says in Isaiah 5:14 that hell has enlarged itself. The Church has strayed from the heart of God; it has gotten so caught up in everything except what God intended. The one great commission to "Go! and Compel them to come," has been moved to the bottom of our lists of things to do … if it's still on our lists at all. People are dying every day and going to an eternal damnation, forever separated from God. And although no one will die without having heard the truth of salvation, the Church is not excused from making the attempt to reach the lost with the message of salvation through Jesus Christ. Where did we go wrong?

After Jesus died and ascended to heaven, He left the apostles with the commission to continue His teachings. As they did, thousands became believers. This was the beginning of the church as we know it. The purpose of the church was to have a place for the new believers in Jesus Christ to go, learn, and grow in this newfound faith.

There were warnings, however, that church leaders were advised to be aware of. The following is a partial teaching from www.gotquestions.org: "In Acts 20:17–38, the apostle Paul has an opportunity to talk to the church leaders in the large city of Ephesus one last time face to face. In that passage, he tells them that false teachers will not only come among them but will come *from* them (vv. 29–30). Paul commits them to the safekeeping of 'God and to the word of His grace" (v. 32). Thus, truth could be determined by depending upon God and "the word of His grace' (i.e., Scripture, see John 10:35). This dependence upon the Word of God, rather than following certain individual "founders" is seen again in Galatians 1:8–9, in which Paul states, 'But even if we, or an angel from heaven, preach any other gospel to you than what we have preached to you, let him be accursed. As we have said before, so now I say again, if anyone preaches any other gospel to you than what you have received, let him be accursed.' Thus, the basis for determining truth from error is not based upon even *who* it is that is teaching it, 'we or an angel from heaven,' but *whether it is the same gospel that they had already received*—and this gospel is recorded in Scripture."

Foundationally, we have compromised and strayed from God's gospel truth. Lies and deceptions have infiltrated the doctrine of God. False teachers are among us, preaching "other gospels." Those who should stand for truth have buckled under the pressure of not being the "odd man out." Other worldly religious groups and beliefs have rallied and protested and fought for equal rights on the basis of freedom of religion and the Church has, as the old saying goes, "turned a blind eye and a deaf ear" for fear of retaliation, for fear of the loss of members, for fear of loss of notoriety, fame, and, in some cases, the almighty dollar.

The twelve apostles would cringe if they were here to witness the apathy of those who are supposed to hold up the bloodstained banner, those who are supposed to still be crying, "Onward Christian soldiers, marching as to war, with the cross of Jesus, going on before!" The church has fallen for the tactics of the enemy, who has caused it to become afraid to "ruffle the feathers" of non-believers.

Acts 4:15–19 says, "But when they had commanded them to go aside out of the council, they conferred among themselves, saying, 'What shall we do to these men? For, indeed, that a notable miracle has been done through them is evident to all who dwell in Jerusalem, and we cannot deny it. But so that it spreads no further among the people, let us severely threaten them, that from now on they speak to no man in this name.'

"So they called them and commanded them not to speak at all nor teach in the name of Jesus. But Peter and John answered and said to them, 'Whether it is right in the sight of God to listen to you more than to God, you judge.'"

In other words, we are going to teach the truth in spite of the possibility of punishment and prison.

And with that, they continued preaching the gospel of Jesus Christ. Acts 5:28–29 says, "And the high priest asked them, saying, 'Did we not strictly command you not to teach in this name? And look, you have filled Jerusalem with your doctrine, and intend to bring this Man's blood on us!' But Peter and the other apostles answered and said: 'We ought to obey God rather than men.'"

They were determined to stand on the truth of the Word of God.

Acts 5:40–41 proves their dogged immovability and focused determination despite the threats to their lives. It says, "and when they had called for the apostles and beaten them, they commanded that they should not speak in the name of Jesus, and let them go. So they departed from the presence of the council, rejoicing that they were counted worthy to suffer shame for His name."

Did you get that? They rejoiced and were glad that they were considered worthy to suffer for the name of Jesus! Who does that?

Where is the Church?

The modern-day church has taken on a "can't we all just get along?" mentality. They don't want to rub anybody the wrong way. They don't want to seem "crazy."

Well, our example was Jesus, who knew that His doctrine would cause contention and division. Matthew 10:34–36 says, "Do not think that I came to bring peace on earth. I did not come to bring peace but a sword. For I have come to 'set a man against his father, a daughter against her mother, and a daughter-in-law against her mother-in-law'; and a man's enemies will be those of his own household."

He knew that His teachings would cause conflict because it was like nothing anybody had ever heard before. Jesus came to break the religious, prideful spirit and to let them know that He was the fulfillment of the Old Testament law. Of course, there would be many who resisted this new doctrine because it was contrary to their pious and religious ways.

Imagine, for a moment, telling people who did not grow up in a Christian home that Jesus is the way. Imagine that they accept this truth and then must go home to what they were raised to believe. Imagine the backlash, the division it would cause.

Jesus still expects us to preach and teach His truth despite the retaliation, hatred, or disagreement that might ensue. Jesus witnessed this Himself, which is why His crucifixion was so horrific. The people were bitter and angry because they could not allow His teachings to undermine and embarrass them.

He even knew His own disciples would run for their lives from fear. He told them in John 16:32, "Indeed the hour is coming, yes, has now come, that you will be scattered, each to his own, and will leave me alone. And yet I am not alone, because the Father is with me. These things I have spoken to you, that in me you may have peace. In the world you will have tribulation; but be of good cheer, I have overcome the world."

He tried to let them know that tribulation would come to those who believe but that His death and resurrection guaranteed their victory in every hostile situation.

He said in I John 3:13, "Do not marvel, my brethren,

if the world hates you." It is not popular to reveal to people that their ways, beliefs, and lives, if not turned to salvation through Jesus, will lead them to an eternity separated from God.

Yet somebody must do it. Somebody must, "by love and kindness, draw them to the Lord." Somebody introduced us to the Lord, and there should continue be that reciprocal effect. We cannot worry about who does not accept it. We are to, "Go and Compel them to come," before it's too late.

In Mark 6:11, Jesus told His disciples, "And whoever will not receive you nor hear you, when you depart from there, shake off the dust under your feet as a testimony against them." Again, they will be without excuse.

Satan is certainly okay with our churches preaching a good Word. He is okay with the great singing and worship and releasing prophetic words. He's okay with you praying and reading the Word of God. He doesn't care how much you go to church or how much money you put in the offering. He doesn't care how much you pray for people or lift your hands in worship.

Don't get me wrong; I'm not knocking these. They are all significant and powerful weapons against him. But what he does not want is souls being saved.

Leading people to salvation through Jesus Christ is snatching them for his own grip. With all the fury and violence he can muster, he forcibly goes against any attempts to reveal God's truth. He savagely revolts against any evangelistic outreach. He uses every evil tactic in his arsenal to deceive many by causing them to focus on everything accept reaching the lost for Christ.

Go ahead and post on social media. Go ahead and have your conferences and prayer calls. Go ahead and preach and baptize. Go ahead and increase your membership. Go ahead and find that comfortable place on the pew at church. Satan is not threatened by that. *He's threatened when the church leaves the building and goes out into the hedges and the highways, compelling the lost to come to Jesus.*

Where is the Church?

For the record, not all churches or ministries have compromised. Some have taken hold and continued the charge to reach the lost for Christ. They are the remnant, the small band of soldiers who are determined, like the apostles, saying, "We ought to obey God rather than men."

Jesus was able to change the world with only twelve. However, it wasn't His intention that we never advance beyond the twelve. *Where is your outreach?*

Where is the Church?

This is not about trying to fill up the church. There is enough of that. How many churches are full, having ten thousand, twenty thousand, or thirty thousand members or more? How many churches have two or three services each Sunday in order to accommodate their enormous congregations?

No, this *is about reaching people and pointing them to salvation. Some people may never set foot in a church.* That doesn't mean they can never have the opportunity to have a relationship with God.

It is sad that many thousands go to church every week; many have sat in the same seat for years and never actually accepted Jesus into their hearts and lives. They are simply churchgoers.

The Bible tells us in Matthew 7:24, "Not everyone who says to Me, 'Lord, Lord,' shall enter the kingdom of heaven, but he who does the will of My Father in heaven."

The surety is in knowing that we have accepted Jesus Christ into our hearts as Savior and that He is Lord of our lives. Getting people to go to church is not sufficient. I have heard so many respond, "But I go to church," when I ask if they have ever accepted Jesus. I have witnessed many come up to the front of the church when the invitation for those who want to rededicate their lives to God is given. When asked why they feel the need to rededicate their lives, they say, "I haven't been to church in a long time."

How many are sitting in your congregations and are simply showing up and occupying a seat from week to week? How many are standing on their feet and lifting their hands and praising God in response to the songs sung and the messages preached yet are still like those in Matthew 7:23, to whom the Lord will say, when they stand before Him on their day of judgment, "Depart from me, I never knew you"? How many run up for prayer and get a prophetic Word but have no relationship with the Lord? They are happy to hear about the great things God has in store for them and walk away with such joy and expectancy, assuming all is well.

Is it though? We are all born with a God-ordained purpose. So, yes, an unsaved person can receive an accurate prophetic Word, but he or she should be made to understand that that purpose is only found and fulfilled via a relationship with God. How many generously give in the offering? How many sit on boards of directors due to status and position in the community but have not been pointed to John 3:3, which says, "Jesus answered and said to him, 'Most assuredly, I say to you, unless one is born again, he cannot see the kingdom of God.'"

There are so many churches that preach a feel-good message weekly; they make people believe that all they have to do is live a good life and do good deeds and be kind and help the less fortunate; they leave people believing that they are okay just because they leave service from week to week feeling positive. The blood of many will be on the hands of those who are lovingly leading them to hell.

Some churches do great things. They feed the hungry, clothe the needy, help build homes for the homeless, donate money to charities. These are all honorable undertakings, but we're meeting a physical need and forgetting or ignoring the spiritual need. Again, the blood of many will be on the hands of those who say they represent Jesus Christ on earth.

Hebrews 13:17 admonishes those in the church to "Obey them that have rule over you, and submit yourselves." Why? Because (it goes on to say) "for they watch for your souls, as they that must give account, that they may do it with joy, and not with grief."

How many are obeying and loyally following those who have rule over them in the Church, yet their souls are still lost? Clearly, there will be grievous accounts to God from leaders as to why they did not effectively watch for the souls of those of whom they were responsible.

Where is the Church?

Chapter 3
Compromise, Deception, and Consequences

What happened to the Church that God built? What happened to God's original intent for His Church? What is the current state of the Church? Somebody has dropped the ball. But is it too late to get the momentum back? What are some of the effects of this falling away? The consequences are clearly devasting. Because the Church has turned a blind eye, it almost seems useless to bother to address it any longer.

The Church seems too far gone and too deeply ingrained in the new freedoms of the world to try to do anything about it. Can God get His Church back to what He originally intended it to be?

Jesus came to seek and save the lost. But so much has changed. It is equivalent to finding a needle in a haystack. The haystack represents the infiltration of everything that is contrary to God's heart. The needle represents the heart of God for His people. How do we find the heart of God in the midst of the deep-rooted mixture in the world today?

The world has been invaded by so many alternative ways of life, so many enticements, so many other interests, all for the purpose of drawing people's attention from their one true need, which is God and Jesus Christ. Gone are the simple days of introducing people to Jesus and getting them to realize that He is the culmination of the fulfillment of their lives. No longer is it simple and easy to get people to understand that, beyond knowing Jesus personally, everything else is secondary.

Of course, the enemy of our souls was not going to sit idly by and not begin his agenda to deceive. He had to use perversion and deception and lies to mislead the masses, as he still does to this day. He had to captivate the imagination by highlighting and shining a light on everything, anything other than God as the priority. It's like dangling a steak in the face of starving people and making them think that this is what they need and need *now* … cast caution and consequences to the wind! He lures them with the enticement that "this" is really what you need, that God has His place but not necessarily in any particular order. Yes, go to church, serve God, but don't ever really make Him Lord of your life. He dangles the money, the jewels, the man, the woman, the drinking, the drugs, the sex, the car, the home, the business, the job, the fame, the fortune, the material gain, etc. in your face. He entrances people and hopes that hold is never broken. He wants people to believe that these things, these endeavors, these pursuits are all they need to have a full life. Why? Because he wants people in hell with him. There's nothing wrong with wanting to live a good life, but at what price? Is it worth the cost of your soul, which Psalm 49 says is "costly"?

Isaiah 46:9–10 says, "I am God, and there is none like me, Declaring the end from the beginning." Well, guess who else is focused more on your end than your beginning? Satan. He knows more about us and God's plans for us than most of us do about ourselves. He knows that we wouldn't be born into this world if God didn't have a purpose for our lives. He knows God's purpose for our lives is great. It frightens him to think we might actually grab hold of and run with it. So, he makes a beeline to disrupt the order that God has for us so that he lead us to a path that is contrary to God's will. All the flashing lights and ringing bells and whistles that he uses throughout our lives are to distract us from what God has for us. *God wants our souls, but so does Satan.* I remember my very first pastor saying that he believed Satan to be so ruthless that if God didn't send His angels to escort our spirits to heaven when we die, Satan would snatch us on the way up. He's ruthless and relentless! That is how serious this is.

But how was he able to begin weaving his web of lies

and deceit with no resistance? Where was the Church? Where were God's representatives? Good questions.

First of all, don't think for one minute that Satan would not consider interrupting God's very own. What better way to cause those who would otherwise believe, to begin to question the genuineness of faith in Jesus Christ, than to paint pictures of doubt in their minds.

In February 2018, a young man shot and killed seventeen people at Marjory Stoneman Douglas High School in Parkland, Florida. One thing stood out to me as the students began to march in protest.

A young lady was livid with those whom she said kept trying to comfort her by saying, "Our thoughts and prayers are with you."

She said, "What good have your thoughts and prayers done?"

I remember thinking, once again, that prayers cannot be isolated to only a time of tragedy. I don't presume to know or judge where people are as far as relationship with the Lord goes, but I do know that as we are not allowed to include the reality of God in our school settings, we can't expect God to jump up and do something at the moment of our tragedies.

There's an old saying: "Lack of preparation on your part does not constitute an emergency on my part." That simply means that just because you fell short somewhere in your responsibility, it doesn't mean that I must suddenly run to your rescue. That's how we look at God sometimes. We keep Him locked away like a genie in a bottle. We keep the bottle safely tucked away or hidden on a shelf or in a closet somewhere. When we find ourselves in some desperate need, we hastily pull the bottle out and frantically rub it because we need our genie to fix it—to make everything all better—right away.

On the other hand, many times there is no consciousness, awareness, or inclusion of God in our lives at all, yet in times of crisis, we want to know why He won't come to our rescue when hell grips our lives. We become angry at this God who is supposed to be good, kind, loving, and caring. What many fail to realize is that God wants relationship. He doesn't want to be called upon only when we're in a fix of some sort. Many question the reality of the truth of the goodness of God because, in their opinion, He didn't come through when they needed Him. Imagine how a parent or friend would feel if you called on them only when there was a desperate need. It's the same with God.

Sadly though, we have to accept that as long as we live in this broken world, there will be heartache and pain, much of which there simply will be no explanation, no answers, or at least answers that make sense. That's just the way it is. There isn't always a reason one person died from cancer but another survived. There aren't always sensible explanations for why this happened to one but not another. We are living in a fallen world. Bottom line: disappointments and brokenness will happen, and we must accept that reality.

When my mother died in 2008, I was angry and sad for a long time because I could not understand why God didn't heal her or at least keep her from suffering. Over the years, I have had to allow God to comfort me and mend my broken heart. I have had to learn to trust the sovereignty of Almighty God. Do I understand now? No. But did I learn to give it all to God and trust Him? Yes. Why? Because God alone is omniscient. He alone is all-knowing.

Additionally, some people associate God with those who are supposed to represent Him. Sadly, they only set themselves up for disappointment when the very ones held in high esteem fall into the sins they preach against. How convenient for the kingdom of darkness.

Remember, Satan, too, is focused on the end of a thing. People who put their faith in the pastor or other church leaders or church members ultimately become part of an overwhelming number of those who fall away from church, from Jesus. Trust slowly dwindles as people feel let down by those who have openly professed their faith and stability in God. How the enemy deceives is by causing people to focus on the sin committed by professed followers of God. But it is never about the sin. It is always about the falling away, about getting people to the point of resolving in their hearts, "I'll never go to church again! I don't trust those church people! I don't believe in God!" When that happens, Satan has won and souls are lost.

In situations like that, we must remind ourselves of what the Bible says in 2 Peter 3:9, "The Lord is not slack concerning His promise, as some count slackness, but is longsuffering towards us, not willing that any should perish but that all should come to repentance."

God never gives up on us. He waits for us to get it together. We are not perfect. However, those who don't know the Lord or who are new in the Lord are not aware of that realization, and we cannot simply let them fall away and become prey for the enemy. We must be like Jesus and leave the ninety-nine to pursue that one lost sheep. There should always be those who refuse to let them drown in discouragement and disappointment, who will throw a lifeline in an effort to reel them in to God's truth.

Many do not realize that their trust should not be solely in a man but in the God that man represents. Somebody must help them understand that, try as we might, we are all fallible human beings. Psalms 103:12 says, "As a father pities his children, So the Lord pities those who fear Him. For He knows our frame; He remembers that we are dust."

We are apt to fall. But we must help them understand that no one is perfect and will sometimes go contrary to

God's will. Nevertheless, God will continue to forgive a repentant heart.

Somehow, we have stayed on the sidelines and watched lives fall away and get lost in the misconception that all churches are bad. We've left people believing that living for Jesus must not really work due to a few who have made mistakes or even misused the name of Jesus and His church. No one escapes. We will all stand before God's judgment seat.

Suicide: A Grave Deception

Another lie the enemy uses to deceive is that when things get bad, there is an easier way out—and that way is to commit suicide.

Again, the enemy is considering the end from the beginning. He is more concerned with the end being an eternity in hell. Suicide is just one way that people are disillusioned into believing they are taking themselves to something better than what they may be currently facing or suffering.

In an episode of the show *Snapped,* a nurse named Charles Cullen, supposedly out of a sense of mercy, killed up to four hundred people. It was reported that he felt he was helping relieve people of their pain. Of course, it turns out he was a mentally ill person, and mercy played no part in these deaths. It was all part of the deception.

The first thought that comes to mind is not that these people died but that he served only to send them to their eternity, ready or not. God forbid many were not saved because, ultimately, he took them from one bad predicament and sent them to their eternal end. There is no coming back. People who say, "Rest in peace," when people die, have no idea that there is no resting in peace for those who die outside of a relationship with the Lord.

Revelation 20:15, in referring to the great white throne judgment, says, "and anyone not found written in the book of Life was cast into the lake of fire." There is no resting in peace for them. Sad but true.

Someone on a local news broadcast recently said, "It's not how a person dies; it's how they lived." Sounds good—but it's far from the truth.

Regardless of how wonderful or even how horrible a person's life is, everyone will die and face God in judgment. The saying should be, "It matters how a person lives, but it matters more how a person dies."

We celebrate the lives of those who live to be ninety or one hundred or older. What a blessing to live to be more than one hundred years old. But what a travesty it is to celebrate such a life only for them to die and face an eternity in hell.

At funerals, it's called a homegoing, or a celebration of life. What home are they going to? Is it really a celebration of life? It is, only if it was a life lived in God. We gaze into a casket that holds the body of the deceased and forget the person we are looking at is no longer present. That person has gone on to face God in judgment.

Hebrews 9:27 says, "And as it is appointed for men to die once, but after this the judgment." What are we (the church) doing to help these people know that suicide doesn't "take them away from their trials and struggles" but only hastens their entry into the face of God's judgment? What are we doing to make sure that when they do die, they are ready to meet God in peace?

Notwithstanding the fact that there are still those who are going to reject the message of salvation through Jesus, again, this does not excuse us from making the attempt to get the good news to them of hope through Jesus Christ.

That is why the Lord tells us in Luke 10:2, "The harvest truly is great, but the laborers are few; therefore, pray for the Lord of the harvest to send out laborers into the harvest."

In other words, the numbers of those who need saving is overwhelming, *but* those who are commissioned to reach them are not very many at all. He goes on to tell us to pray for laborers. How many prayers have I heard where people say, "Lord, here I am, send me"? Oddly though, when the call comes to "go," only one or two seem willing, if that many. Imagine how that breaks God's heart.

Where is the Church?

Because many in the world today resist and reject Jesus as "the Way," so many Christians have retreated and gone into hiding. Many feel as though it is just not worth the fight. Many do not want to deal with the backlash, hatred, disagreement, and retaliation that comes as a result of standing on the truth of God's Word.

In Luke 10:3, the Lord even prepares them by making it clear to "Go your way; behold, I send you out as lambs among wolves." He tells us in John 15:18–20, "If the world hates you, you know that it hated me before it hated you. If you were of the world, the world would love its own. Yet because you are not of the world, but I chose you out of the world, therefore the world hates you. Remember the word that I said to you, 'A servant is not greater than his master.' If they persecuted me, they will also persecute you."

And again, remember that He tells us to not fear but to be at peace. In John 16:33, the Lord says, "These things I have spoken to you, that in me you may have peace. In the world you will have tribulation, but be of good cheer, I have overcome the world."

Just as no one will have an excuse when they stand before the judgment seat of Christ, so are we, who know the truth, without excuse. We are to be the laborers who go after the plenteous harvest that is before our very eyes. Though we have been hearing and believing for thousands of years that Jesus is coming again, it does not negate the truth that He is coming again, be it today, tomorrow, or in another thousand years. Our mandate is to obey His command, as Luke 14:23 says, to "go out into the highways and hedges and compel them to come in"—"*go out*" being the operative phrase here.

But we have excuses, one being, "I'm not called as an evangelist." Yes, of course not all are called to the office of the evangelist, but we are *all* called to share the gospel with others. We are, indeed, without excuse.

Where is the Church?

Chapter 4
Internal Sabotage

Sabotage is defined in Miriam Webster's dictionary as "an act or process of tending to hamper or hurt." Sabotage is one of Satan's main weapons in his arsenal against the people of God. To make matters worse, he uses those inside the church, who are professed Christians, to sabotage the very work and Word of God. Hence, the internal sabotage. I said earlier that he doesn't have to lift a finger, because he sits back and watches us destroy each other. Planted among the members are those who knowingly and sometimes unknowingly cause division and corruption in the church.

There are also those, as I stated earlier, who begin to release a contrary gospel. Again, in Galatians 1:8-9, Paul states, "But even if we, or an angel from heaven, preach any other gospel to you than what we have preached to you, let him be accursed."

For example, who remembers Reverend Ike? When

I was a child I remembered the excitement over his "prayer cloths." Many people right in my neighborhood purchased them because they supposedly healed and brought wealth. According to his Wikipedia entry: "When it came to the worship of mammon, Rev. Ike was as transparent as they came. "It is the *lack* of money that is the root of all evil," he used to say. "The best thing you can do for the poor is not to be one of them." Decades ahead of Oprah Winfrey and the author of *The Secret* in the mainstreaming of greed as a middle-class virtue, Rev. Ike's theology was indistinguishable from the fever dream of the most unrepentant capitalist: "Forget about the pie-in-the-sky; get yours here and now."

Those of us who know God's Word know that it says in 1 Timothy 6:10, "For the love of money is the root **of** all evil: which while some coveted after, they have erred from the faith, and pierced themselves through with many sorrows."

Of course, Reverend Ike distorted this truth and won over millions of people. I don't ever remember him preaching on the salvation of the soul. I distinctly remember his huge personality drawing people into his prosperity preaching. People sent him their rent money because they believed in Reverend Ike's message of "getting the pie in the sky right now." One preacher put it this way: "Get your steak on the plate while you wait." Reverend Ike misquoted the scripture, "the love of money is the root of all evil."

God is very clear about how the single pursuit of riches and wealth will cause a person to lose what is most precious—his or her soul.

Another example of internal sabotage is the Reverend Carlton Pearson who, in recent years, came up with the term "universal reconciliation." According to Wikipedia, it is defined as "the doctrine that all sinful and alienated human souls—because of divine love and mercy—will ultimately be reconciled to God.

The doctrine has generally been rejected by Christian religions, which hold to the doctrine of special salvation that, only some members of humanity will eventually enter heaven, but it has received support from many prestigious Christian thinkers, as well as many groups of Christians.

Note the last line, which says, "it has received support from many prestigious Christian thinkers, as well as groups of Christians."

God warned us in Mark 13:22 that in end times, even the elect could possibly be deceived. It says, "For false christs and false prophets will rise and show signs and wonders to deceive, if possible, even the elect."

None of what is happening in our world and in our time is news. There have been and will be many more who will come with contrary teachings. They too will have to answer to God.

Revelation 22:19 says, "If anyone adds to these things, God will add to him the plagues that are written in this book; and if anyone takes away from the words of the book of this prophecy, God will take away his part from the book of Life, from the holy city, and from the things that are written in this book."

There are so many who are being deceived, and it is up to us, God's church, to get the truth to them. I have students who have never even seen a Bible. My copy sat on my desk, and I've had students ask, "What is that?"

I say, "It's my Bible."

They reply, "You read that thing?"

I say, "Well, yes."

And they are amazed. There are more than we know who either don't know the truth or believe they know the truth when they don't. Others just don't know what the truth really is.

Where is the Church?

We must help people understand that personal opinions do no matter. It does not matter if we agree or not. God is not after our approval or agreement.

Romans 3:3–4 says, "For what if some did not believe? Will their unbelief make the faithfulness of God without effect? Certainly not! Indeed, let God be true but every man a liar."

It doesn't matter if we say we don't believe God's Word. Nowhere in scripture do we read where God stops as He is creating the world and asks, "Is this okay? Is it okay with you mere mortals, you human beings, for me, the God of the universe, to do this or say that?" No!

The Bible makes it very clear that there would be such heresy in our times. God warns us about that again and again in scripture. It bears repeating: "But even if we, or an angel from heaven, preach any other gospel to you than what we have preached to you, let him be accursed." Galatians 1:8-9

Believe me, I do realize how incomprehensible it is for our finite, human minds to accept the notion of an eternal conscious torment. It is much too overwhelming to grasp the realization that a loving God would allow that to happen to fallible human beings.

Yet the fact remains that we are either going to accept the Word of God as it is or not at all. We cannot take the parts we agree with or the parts we like, and smile, as if that is enough. It is literally all or nothing. We don't have to like it. We don't have to agree. God is not moved by our sense of unsettling where His Word is concerned. He does, however, allow us the right to choose.

In Deuteronomy 30:15–19, He says, "See, I have set before you today life and good, death and evil, in that I command you today to love the Lord your God, to walk in His ways, and to keep His commandments,

His statutes, and His judgments, that you may live and multiply and the Lord your God will bless you in the land which you go to possess. But if your heart turns away so that you do not hear, and are drawn away, and worship other gods and serve them, I announce to you today that you shall surely perish.

I call heaven and earth as witnesses today against you, that I have set before you life and death, blessing and cursing; therefore, choose life, that both you and your descendants may live."

As horrible as it is to consider hell, God still provides a way of escape, a way to spend eternity with Him.

God is sovereign. He knew there would be some who would deceive and those who would fall for the lie. In Galatians 3, the apostle Paul speaks to the church in Galatia when He says in verse 1: "O foolish Galatians! Who has bewitched you that you should not obey the truth, before whose eyes Jesus Christ was clearly among you as crucified? This only I want to learn from you: Did you receive the Spirit by the works of the law, or by the hearing of faith? Are you so foolish? Having begun in the Spirit, are you now being made perfect by the flesh? Have you suffered so many things in vain—if indeed it was in vain?"

God knew there would be those who would creep into the church and begin to spread lies. He also knew there would be those who would fall for the lies. Again, it's all about the falling away.

No matter how people have tried, Christianity can never be overthrown. Their final option has been to attempt to sabotage it through a mixing of lies with God's truth. This incorporation of deception with truth has negatively affected many of those who once believed. Second Timothy 4:3 tells us, "For the time will come when they will not endure sound doctrine, but according to their own desires, because they have itching ears, they will heap up for themselves teachers; and they will turn their ears away from the truth and be turned aside to fables."

Jesus said in Mark 13:22 that "False christs and false prophets will rise and show signs and wonders to deceive, if possible, even the elect." In Matthew 24:11, Jesus says, "Then many false prophets will rise up and deceive many."

This is nothing new to the Lord. He has tried to warn us so we don't fall for the lie. By nature, we want something that makes us feel good. We want something that doesn't convict us or cause us to be accountable for our actions. By nature, we want to live and do as we please with no consequences. We want God to be all accepting and loving in spite of our behaviors and actions. If there really is any truth to God being a righteous God who judges sin, we want no part of it. God *is* loving, but He also established His expectations of His created ones. He has given us a choice. We must choose. No one escapes.

Intellectually and scientifically this makes no sense to us. But it is fruitless to attempt to understand God with our minds and emotions. The Bible says, God is a Spirit and those who worship Him but worship Him in Spirit and in truth—not in our personal thoughts and feelings about Him. Try as we might, God and His Word will never make sense in the natural sense of things or through our intellect.

Second Corinthians 2:14 says, "But the natural man does not receive the things of the Spirit of God, for they are foolishness to him; nor can he know them, because they (God's Words) are spiritually discerned (understood)." First Corinthians 1:18 says, "For the message of the cross is foolishness to those who are perishing, but to us who are being saved it is the power of God."

Simply put, we cannot understand God outside of a personal relationship with Him. We receive the Spirit of God when we are saved. Beyond that experience, one is left to try to decipher God with the natural mind, which we now know is impossible.

Again we, the church, do not have to stand idly by and allow this deception to spread like a plague. Some people really do not know any better. Some do not realize they have fallen into a trap. We have the responsibility to battle against and defeat the lies of hell. We must speak up and respond to the lies of the devil, our rebuttal being the truth of God's Word.

Second Corinthians 4:3 says, "But even if our gospel is hid, it is hid to those who are perishing, whose minds the god of this world has blinded, who do not believe, lest the light of the gospel of the glory of Christ, who is the image of God, should shine on them." If we do not speak up, those very ones who are perishing will be forever lost in the blindness and darkness of Satan's lies.

Second Corinthians 4:6 completes what is expected of us by offering hope: "For it is the God who commanded light to shine out of darkness, who has shone in our hearts to give the light of the knowledge of the glory of God in the face of Jesus Christ."

In other words, when we speak the truth of the Word of God, God shines His light into the darkness that has blinded those who are perishing, thereby offering them the hope of salvation. So many professed Christians have fallen into the enticement of Satan's schemes. They have allowed their souls to question God's truth and are now spreading it across the land as gospel.

We must know by now that nothing is beyond or beneath Satan. He stops at nothing to deceive, even if it means stepping right in the middle of the church and between God's people. This is exactly what is meant by giving us enough rope to hang ourselves. He stands by and watches the church become like a circus, and he laughs.

This adds a new perspective on considering the need

for salvation. Salvation is clearly more than the initial saving of the soul. Those of us who are saved need to also pray and intercede for those who are of the faith, because Satan clearly has no bounds. He honestly is the accuser of the brethren.

We need to pray for judgment upon those who are causing discord and division within God's church. We need to pray for those who are being drawn away from God's truth. Remember, it is not about what a person like Rev. Ike, Carlton Pearson, Jim Jones, David Koresh, or Warren Jeffs have done, it's about the falling away of those who belong to the kingdom of God. It is about the souls that will be lost due to the lies and the deception of our enemy, Satan.

It can't be repeated enough: Satan's one goal, his one agenda is to take as many to hell with him as he can. Remember that. He is pulling out all the stops. He's using every avenue he can to steal, kill, and destroy. He has to be dramatic; he has to go over the top; he has to use all the bells and whistles to get people's attention away from God. Otherwise, people would just shoo him away like a pesky bug. He has to use elaborate tactics to woo people into his wicked web.

For example, as of late, there is this new phenomenon called "the church of Beyoncé." It is a new cult, offering a mixture of religious freedom and the music of Beyoncé to draw in the masses. And it's working. Instead of those who know the Lord going into prayer for those souls, most are jumping on the bandwagon of unleashing word curses against them, all in the name of holiness. We must be careful not to get caught up in the hype. We must not put our mouths on people along with those who don't know the Lord. These are souls that God is still not willing should perish. God is still saying He wants all people everywhere to be saved. Pray, people of God, pray! Believe God to intercept the lie and draw these people to his truth. We need God to heal our land! Do you remember "If my people ...?"

Still needed are those who will stand up and represent the God of heaven, the God who sent His Son, that whosoever believes in Him will not perish but have everlasting life. God is saying, "Who will go for me?" He is still looking for those who will stand in the gap. He is still listening for those who will say, "Here am I, Lord, send me." If we cannot physically go, we can go in prayer and intercession. But we must *go*!

Where is the Church?

Can somebody say, "*Wake up, Church!*"? What are we doing while all the plans of the enemy seem to be flourishing? Is there anything too hard for God? Do we still believe that? Or are we like the cowardly lion in the movie *The Wizard of Oz* as he cries, 'Somebody pulled my tail," not realizing that he is pulling his own tail. Have we taken hold of fear and intimidation so much that we are crying, "Somebody pulled my tail"? Do we not realize that as we stand back and do nothing, we are, because of fear, pulling our own tails and allowing the enemy to rule and reign on earth?

Psalm 115:16 says, "The heaven, even the heavens are the Lord's; But the earth He has given to the children of men." It was God's intention from the beginning of time, from the creation of the world, that we have dominion. In Genesis 1:28 God said, "have dominion over all." Have we really given up our dominion?

One description in the Bible for Satan is the "prince of the power of the air." Like radio waves, he releases mind-binding lies into the minds of people while we … do what? It seems we, God's church, have gotten to a place of hopelessness. It does seem no use to try because the state of our world is so dark. The demonic world has gotten such a stronghold on a great majority of people that we, God's church, seem to have taken on a posture of defeatism. The mind-set of the church seems to be, "What's the use?" I'm sure most question any attempt to combat it due to impending backlash and retaliation from those who stand firm in their contrary beliefs.

In the movie *The Martian*, Matt Damon is stranded on Mars after his crew leaves him, assuming he is dead. After a few months into their trip back to Earth, they learn from Mission Control that he is still alive. To return for him would be a nearly three-year journey. They could have said, "It's too late; it's too dangerous; he's just one man, and we can do without him. He may be dead by the time we get back to him." Ultimately, they go back and are miraculously able to save him.

Have we, as the church of God, looked at the condition of the world and said, "What can we do? It's too much; it's too late; the depravity is too deeply rooted and the world is too far sunken into sin; it's too dangerous; they're already lost; forget them." Is anything too hard for God? Who will go back for them so they may be saved?

Where is the Church?

Chapter 5
Social Media

Years ago, the only mode of getting the word out was to actually walk from door to door. Now, it is so easy to reach the masses. Radio and television was once the be-all and end-all, but the creation of computers, tablets, and cell phones has opened multiple avenues to reach people. Facebook and Instagram, to name a couple, have allowed opportunities for online ministry—for free! There are people who will never and have never set foot into a church building but will listen to a message released through social media. Some ministers testify to followers they have never met in person.

It would be too good to be true to not have the interference from the one who conveniently mixes his lies in with the truth that is intended to be released through social media. Satan has nothing to use of his own. He can only copy or mimic yet ultimately corrupt what God has meant for our good. How does he do that?

Very subtly! I don't know how true it is, but I have heard that a lobster is slowly boiled to death. It has no idea when it is first placed in the water that its demise is slow but sure. As the water temperature heats up, the lobster gradually adjusts to it, all the while heading to its last breath.

This mirrors how the enemy behaves. He lures people via means of what appears innocent. He draws people into his subtle lies. He twists truths or offers convenient alternatives to truths through subliminal messages and stories that we see on TV or at the movies or on social media posts.

You hear, through movies, stories of people who die and are depicted as going to "a better place." In the movie *Armageddon,* Bruce Willis's character has to make the hard decision to stay behind in order to detonate a meteor that would otherwise destroy Earth. He gets the opportunity to say goodbye to his daughter and says, "I'm afraid I'll have to break the promise I made to you. It looks like I won't be coming home." He goes on to say, "But I'll be looking down on you …"

There's nothing wrong with that … nothing at all. But again, it leaves the general public to fall into the trap that all people who die go to "a better place." That is simply not the truth.

There are movies where topics that would normally be taboo or seem suspicious are portrayed as "fun," "kind," or "loving." These topics are transformed into a comedy, and we miss the fact that something demonic has totally gone over our heads. We're too busy laughing and not realizing that this is the enemy's attempt to desensitize us to things we would normally be leery of. It is the proverbial lobster being slowly cooked to death.

And then suddenly, nothing is off limits; everything is acceptable. People become like zombies, all the while being led into a trap. At some point, the lines of good and evil, right and wrong, acceptable and unacceptable become so blurred that two become one and there just is no "wrong" anymore. The line of demarcation has been erased, and people end up walking, eyes wide open, into hell.

So many are on social media, and so many falsehoods are released for the purpose to deceive. For every truth of God, there are many more posts mixed with information to lead people astray. People are left wondering what to believe. It is human nature to want the easy way, to want the road most traveled, to want the way of least resistance. Where does that leave us as the church of God?

People don't want to feel stifled; they don't want to feel like they have been placed in a box deprived of their freedom. By nature, we want to live and let live; we want to "have our cake and eat it too," as the saying goes; we want to live precariously yet be accountable to no one. Yet at the end of our lives, we want to believe that we will "rest in peace."

We, as God's truth bearers, must help people understand that as binding as God's Word seems, it indeed is the only way. We must let them know that God's Word says in Matthew 7:13–14, "Enter by the narrow gate; for wide is the gate and broad is the way that leads to destruction, and there are many who go in by it. Because narrow is the gate and difficult is the way which leads to life, and there are few who find it."

This is God's way. It literally means that many are following the popular way but that way leads to death—to hell. The way to eternal life is narrow; it's hard, and few go that way because it goes against everything that comes naturally to us in our minds and emotions. As hard as that is, we must still reach out to people and help them understand that they must still choose, and if they choose what's contrary to God's way, they are choosing an end separated from God for all eternity.

We can't worry about whether or not we will offend. It has been made very clear that Jesus offended many. His one focus was saving people's souls and letting them know they must choose. Many resented His teachings, but He completed what He was sent to the world to accomplish. And so must we.

Remember, the Bible says hell has enlarged itself. Why? Because many are choosing the wide gate that leads them there. The wide gate is the one that requires no accountability for one's actions; it is the one that leaves people saying, "It matters not how one dies but how one lives." This too is another tactic of the enemy to desensitize people and leave them believing that anything goes, and even more so that in the end, all will be well.

The enemy tricks people into believing that all they need to do is live a good, honest, and decent life; he makes them believe that if they are good-hearted and giving, everything will turn out all right.

A former supervisor of mine became irate with me years ago when I tried to explain salvation to him. He kept saying, "You mean to tell me that God would send me to hell even though I'm a good person?" He could not fathom that a loving God would do that to a person such as himself.

In all honesty, he really was a good person. There was nothing he wouldn't do for you. He was very nice and giving and understanding. Remember how scripture says that the things of God are foolishness to those who are perishing. So of course it would make no sense to him to consider that he could go to hell though he was a "good person."

What must we do as the people of God? We must teach them that we are born sinners, that we inherited this sin nature from Adam and Eve. It is no different than inheriting our hair color or disposition or attitudes or tone of voice from our parents. When Adam and Eve sinned, their sin nature passed to all human beings.

We must share the Word in Ephesians 2:8–9 that says, "For by grace you have been saved through faith, and that not of yourselves; it is the gift of God, not of works, lest anyone should boast." Romans 5 explains to us how "one man's disobedience caused many to be made sinners." We must help people understand that no one is "good enough" to deserve heaven. We're born with a need for a savior. All we can do is tell the truth and pray for the Holy Spirit to draw them to God.

It is unthinkable that people who have done good deeds or given noble service or lived as basically good people could actually die and go to hell. On Memorial Day, we hear all the expressions of praise and thanksgiving offered to veterans. We're reminded to thank them for serving for our country. We thank the ones who died years earlier for giving their lives for us. Think about people like Mahatma Gandhi, Mother Theresa, or Princess Diana. What about the pope? Consider great minds such as John Nash, Stephen Hawking, and Albert Einstein. What about popular officials like presidents of the United States? What about Muhammad Ali, Michael Jackson, Prince, and the like? Is it possible that these, who have represented the finest of society, could die and go to an eternal conscious torment? They were enormous personalities. They accomplished great things. They were "good" people. What about those who were not so good, like Fidel Castro, Saddam Hussein, Osama bin Laden, and Adolf Hitler, to name a few? These are the ones whom we are sure have gone to hell because they were horrible people. But (and there's always a but) good or bad or somewhere in between, when they all, good or bad or somewhere in between, took their last breaths, when they went to stand before the judgment seat of Christ, did God say, "Depart from me, I never knew you"?

Ephesians 2:8 says, "For by grace you have been saved through faith, and that not of yourselves: it is a gift of God, not of works, lest anyone should boast."

There is nothing we can or need to do to earn our way into heaven. It is a gift that we accept by faith.

In a nutshell, what matters is whether or not they knew Jesus Christ as the Savior and Lord of their lives. That is man's all. Matthew 16:26 says, "For what profit is it to a man if he gains the whole world, and loses his soul? Or what will a man give in exchange for his soul?" The Word of God confirms over and over that Jesus is the Son of God. (Read, for example, John 20:31, 1 Corinthians 1:9, 1 John 4:14–15.) As an example, Muslims, like Muhammad Ali, do not believe or accept Jesus as the Son of God. I'll leave you with that.

Those of us who know better must do better. We must do better, even if it's at the expense of making a few enemies. We must do so at the expense of the angry disagreement that may be directed toward us. Now we have a choice whether we say, "We ought to obey God rather than men." We have a choice now to say like Peter and Paul in Acts 4, "Whether it is right in the sight of God to listen to you more than to God, you judge." Only God will judge us when we stand before Him, but there are many thousands dying daily who honestly believe they are okay and will leave this life and rest in peace. Many are severely disillusioned by this notion. Someone must tell them.

Where is the Church?

At this juncture in life, Satan is sitting back and watching church members combat and destroy each other. He causes us to disagree on topics like whether or not there are people in heaven and hell now or whether everyone is decomposing in the grave. This is one of his subtle ways to accomplish his mission of confusing and distracting the masses.

He uses many other schemes to cause the churches of God to destroy each other. He watches and laughs, I'm sure, as we disagree on things like whether women should be allowed to preach, whether women should wear pants, whether there are modern-day apostles and prophets, or whether that ended in biblical times, whether God still heals (or was that something that happened only when Jesus was on earth), whether we should worship on Saturday or Sunday, whether we should tithe, whether speaking in tongues is still relevant or was it only a one-time deal on the day of Pentecost, whether Jesus was white or black—the list goes on and on. Yet we all say we abide by the same Word of God. Satan will stop at nothing to cause us to miss this one important fact: to accept Jesus Christ as Savior of our lives.

Some will be so busy disagreeing and arguing about such trivial issues that they'll miss the one reason that matters most to God. They will stand before the throne of judgment trying to figure out how they missed it. Satan knows that his fate is sealed. He knows he will burn in the lake of fire and brimstone for all eternity. He's determined, however, to not go alone.

Where is the Church?

Chapter 6
To Go or Not to Go? That Is the Question

Church has become such big business now. Preachers on TV or social media barely get into their sermons or messages before their latest books or CDs or DVDs are presented for sale. Yes, of course the Bible says that a laborer is worthy of his hire. Public ministry is how many make their living, and there's nothing wrong with that. But where do we draw the line between making a living and totally forgetting that there are lost souls in the world? When do we remember that there are those who are not saved and will not be watching your show on Christian TV networks? Your books and CDs and DVDs are for those who are already saved. Though not impossible, it is very unlikely that unsaved people are going to buy a book on "how to get saved." Go make your living from your book, CD, and DVD sales. Some have become very rich and popular because of their broad ministry reach. But God still says that we must *go* ... we must *go … we must go …* "into the hedges and highways and compel them to come in" (Luke 14:23). We must *go* "into all the world and preach the gospel to every creature" (Matthew 16:7). Otherwise, we will continue to miss opportunities to share the truth of salvation and many more will end up lost in hell. "*We*" must go! "*We* must go!*" "*We!*" That's "us!" You and I!

Where is the Church?

We are constantly praying against the spirit of fear and intimidation when it comes to someone walking out God's call on his or her life. It seems we may have to continue to pray the same, considering today's state of outreach in most churches. Again, a big majority have fallen subject to fear of backlash and have become intimidated by impending retaliation from those who do not agree with the gospel we are called to support and preach. God already made it very clear that there will be those who reject His gift of salvation no matter how plain and simple His message of love is expressed.

God commanded Ezekiel to speak His words to the people although He already knew they would reject it. In Ezekiel 2:7, God tells him, "You shall speak My words to them whether they hear or whether they refuse, for they are rebellious." He further commanded him in 3:11: "And go, get to the captives, to the children of your people, and speak to them and tell them, 'Thus says the Lord God, whether they hear, or whether they refuse.'"

How much clearer can God be? It is not about trying to "make" people accept His truth; it is about ensuring that they hear His truth, that they know that there is an alternative, there is a choice that they must make, "whether they hear or whether they refuse."

Sadly, hell will not be empty, due to those who are already there and those who will go. In spite of every effort on our part, in spite of God's agape love for humankind, some will still refuse to believe.

Matthew 24:37–38, though a New Testament scripture, points out the similarities in our days with the fate of those who refused to believe Noah's warnings. It says, "But as the days of Noah were, so also will the coming of Son of Man be. For as in the days before the flood, they were eating and drinking, marrying, and giving in marriage, until the day Noah entered the ark, and did not know until the flood came and took them all away, so also will the coming of the Son of Man be."

Though Noah forewarned the people of the impending doom, though he offered them a chance to repent, they only jeered and laughed at him, thinking him foolish.

So it is today. Truth be told, no matter how far our outreach goes, some are going to reject it and ultimately select an eternity separated from God. (We can read Nehemiah 9 for a greater understanding of the extensive patience of God.) But time will run out and it will be too late.

To further illustrate the extreme depravity of the heart of mankind and the severity of the deception from the enemy, let's revisit Luke 16, where it describes the beggar Lazarus's death and entry into Abraham's bosom and the death of the rich man, at whose gate Lazarus would lie down and beg. This rich man went to hell. While in torment, the rich man saw Abraham far off and cried out, begging Abraham to send Lazarus with water to cool his tongue from the torment of the flames. Of course, that was not going to happen. Suddenly, the rich man remembered that he had five brothers who, if they didn't turn to the Lord, would find themselves facing the same torment.

Case in point: 27–31 says, "Then he said, 'I beg you therefore, father, that you would send him (Lazarus) to my father's house, for I have five brothers, that he may testify to them, lest they also come to this place of torment. Abraham said to him, 'They have Moses and the prophets; let them hear them.' And he said, 'No, father Abraham; but if one goes to them from the dead, they will repent.' But he said to him, 'If they do not hear Moses and the prophets, neither will they be persuaded though one rise from the dead.'"

Are you seeing this? There will be some who simply will not repent and turn to God. Horrifying to think about, isn't it? Are we excused from making the attempt to reach them? By now you know the answer to that.

Where is the Church?

Why does God specifically use the word "go" before certain scriptures? Why didn't he just say, in Luke 14:23, "Compel them to come"? Why didn't He just say, in Matthew 8:19, "Make disciples of all men"? Why didn't He just say, in Ezekiel 3:4, "Speak My words to the house of Israel," or in verse 11, "Speak to them and tell them"? Why didn't He just say, in Mark 16:15, "preach the gospel to every creature"? Why didn't he say in Isaiah 6:9, "Tell these people!" Each of these verses lead with the word "Go!"

Today, we have people who compel them to come; they are making disciples; they are speaking God's words; they are telling people; they are preaching the gospel. Most, however, are making these attempts by way of TV, radio, or social media platforms. But who is still physically "going"? Yes, these are modern times, and yes, there are other ways of going, but what about the ones who will not tune in to any religious programming whatsoever? What about those who will not buy your book? What about those who will never set foot inside a church? What about those who have not heard? God still says, "Go," to those who use social media as their way of excuse, as a way of saying they just have a different way of going, for the purpose of quieting a real conviction from the Lord to get out there.

The enemy has taken control of the mountain of arts

and entertainment and various forms of media. There are so many TV programs that cause the subconscious mind to believe that anything goes. No subject is off limits. Nothing causes us to question the morality of topics that would have been shameful to discuss years ago. We are reeled in and unknowingly fall into the trance of approval and acceptance. The message comes across as, "That's not so bad." We are fooled into feeling like we are discriminating against people due to our belief in the Word of God. There are shows sporting everything that God says no to. We must be careful because there is a clear difference between approval and acceptance. There are issues that we accept but do not necessarily approve of. But in the things of God, we must not find ourselves compromising God's truth.

Movies and video games also target our minds and consciences. Because we have, in so many ways, blended in with what's popular, we have lost our voices, where the line has been crossed between good and evil. Those of us who know the Lord and have been properly educated in the Word of God fare better and are safer from distractions and deceptions.

But what about those who don't know the Lord, who don't go to church, who have been brought up one way, believing one thing, not realizing that there is a God way?

Much of the popular secular music is full of mind-binding lies of Satan. Is it good music? Yes! Is most of it designed to draw the mind and soul into a place of spiritual bondage? Yes! Satan has no bounds, remember? He will stop at nothing to lock people into a prison of blindness and deafness to God's truth. They don't realize they are bound and that they need Jesus. We must "go" and tell them. The message of Jesus's salvation won't reach them if we don't take it to them. Some have heard the truth and ignored it for various reasons, but we still need to be the ones who water the seeds already planted.

Chapter 7
Evangelizing the Church

How many of us, honestly, came to the Lord at the first mention of salvation through Jesus? Or how many of us came to Jesus and never strayed?

With that in mind, how many are already in the church, so to speak, and are still not in a sold-out relationship with the Lord? Evangelism is not only reaching the unsaved. Sometimes outreach must be done right inside the church. The need to evangelize the "churched" is also of utmost importance. Many accept Jesus Christ, but that is the extent of it. They are basically receiving what has been termed "fire insurance." They had a surreal moment (or in some instances, moments) and realized that they didn't want to go to hell. In a fit of emotion, they prayed to accept Jesus Christ into their hearts.

Churches are full of church members who never progress to anything more. How many people have been members of their churches for years and years, who are very active in the church, who give faithfully in the offering, who sit on boards of directors, who are heads of teams or auxiliaries, but whose lives have never actually been converted into a true relationship with God? How many pastors or leaders of churches will stand before God, having the blood of many souls on their hands, knowing that they allowed these people to sit in their congregations, never having urged them to live a life that is pleasing and acceptable to God? Yes, yes, yes, people do have a choice, but some are sitting in otherwise "dead churches," attending week after week, where the only absent one is the Holy Spirit. These congregants are dying spiritually and don't realize it. They go through the motions of an emotional church experience; they follow the program when, all the while, God is after their hearts and lives. God wants relationship, but that is nonexistent. These types of churches have been said to have what is called an "Ichabod" spirit—Ichabod meaning "the spirit of the Lord has departed." Evangelism is clearly an active need in many local churches.

How is it that I know this? Because at one point in my life, I too went to church when the doors opened. Other than that, I lived my life and did everything I wanted to do because I had not totally surrendered to God. The difference, though, is that I was at a church where right living was taught. The Word of God was made clear, and we were admonished to live according to it because we had now accepted Jesus as Savior. It took me years and years … and more years to finally get to a place where I wanted to live completely for God.

God is our heavenly Father. Just as our natural parents want more than a weekly hello from us, so does God, our heavenly parent. He wants a relationship. Many never attain that place of genuine relationship because it is very costly. Some also feel that such a relationship is too restricting. That is why the Bible says, "few there be that find the way to eternal life."

Another major concern in the church is the oblivion to those who are saved but still hurting, broken, discouraged, angry, or despondent. They love the Lord; they have given their all to Him, yet they have not been set free from old bondages, disappointments, losses, or devastations they experienced before they came to know the Lord. Beyond salvation, the Lord wants us free and whole. He really does want us to experience the "life more abundantly" that the Bible tells us about. These believers are active and even productive but are bound. They are existing but not living. They are functioning daily but are still tied to and essentially harassed and tormented mentality and emotionally by what used to be. This is why some slowly fade away, leaving the church and even slipping back into the life they lived outside of God. They've never been taught how to "cast all their cares upon the Lord." They have never been delivered from former pains, soul ties, heartaches, and any other things that keep them captive. Many have become experts at wearing masks. Physically, they look and act as if all is well. And the truth is, some have no idea that there are lingering attachments from the enemy. They have no idea that they even need deliverance. Others are tormented and do not know why. Even worse, we miss it. We leave them in survival mode when God has said that He wants them free … and free indeed.

Where is the Church?

Chapter 8
Once Saved, Always Saved?

Have you heard the old adage, "Once saved, always saved?" Much controversy has been thrown around concerning this saying. It is a very touchy subject, because how can a saved person lose his or her salvation? It has been said by some that perhaps it is not that people can lose their salvation but perhaps the truth is that they were never really saved at all.

What about those who honestly and sincerely accepted Jesus at one point but never moved into a deeper knowledge of who God wanted to be in their lives? They are the ones who received the fire insurance. Are they saved for real? I believe they are.

But consider those who grew into a true son/daughter relationship with God, those whose lives exemplify what God will be looking for when Jesus returns to rapture His church out of the world.

Ephesians 5:27 tells us how Christ wants to be able

to present His church "not having spot or wrinkle or any such thing, but that she should be holy and without blemish." 2 Peter 3:14 says, "Therefore, beloved, looking forward to these things, be diligent to be found by Him in peace, without spot and blameless."

Doesn't that sound as if there are some stipulations, some rules, some expectations from the Lord as to who will be acceptable for His glorious heaven? How can one live a life unto oneself and still expect to be received into heaven?

Again, some say, perhaps they were never really saved. But there really was a genuine change of heart; there was a sincere cry to the Lord for His salvation.

At one point in my walk with the Lord, I continued to go to the night clubs and drink alcohol and smoke weed and have sex outside of marriage. I lied and cheated and stole. I still liked some people and didn't like others. I still gossiped and had bad attitudes. I was still deceptive and dishonest and decided what part of the Bible I would live by and what parts I would not. All the while, I was still sitting in Bible study, teaching Sunday school and singing in the choir.

Was I just never saved? Oh, but I was. There was just no conviction in my heart for what I was doing. At some point I had to come to a place of grieving over the life I was living because it was not pleasing to God. Some never get to that place. Some continue to have no conscience about the way they live their lives; they have no sense of the heart of God, and they never change.

When a person like that dies, do they go to heaven? When Jesus returns, will that person be "caught up to meet the Lord in the air"? Or are they left behind? Consider the difference between the ones who haphazardly live a life of their own accord even after accepting Jesus as opposed to those who sell out to the Lord and live as much as possible within the bounds of the Word of God.

The Bible says in Matthew 7:21–23, "Not everyone who says to me, 'Lord, Lord,' shall enter the kingdom of heaven, but he who does the will of my Father in heaven. Many will say to me in that day, 'Lord, Lord have we not prophesied in Your name, cast out demons in Your name, and done many wonders in Your name?' And then I will declare to them, 'I never knew you; depart from me, you who practice lawlessness!'"

Correct me if I'm wrong, but these are those who are of the family of God who clearly misrepresented God and His Word. The above scripture refers to those who will say that they cast out demons in Jesus's name. Think about it. You cannot cast out demons without the spirit of the Lord living within you. So they are clearly saved.

In Matthew 12:24, when Jesus cast a demon out of a man, it says, "Now when the Pharisees heard it they said, "This fellow does not cast out demons except by Beelzebub, the ruler of the demons." But Jesus answers him by saying in verse 26, "If Satan casts out Satan, he is divided against himself. How then will his kingdom stand?"

Verse 28 says, "But if I cast out demons by the Spirit of God, surely the kingdom of God has come upon you."

In other words, a demon would not cast out a demon. Why would it want to? That wouldn't make sense, right? Only the spirit of God in a person can cast out or would want to cast out a demon. The verse in Matthew 7 is clearly speaking of those who are saved and have cast out demons in Jesus's name and have prophesied in His name. It is to these, Jesus says, "Depart from me, I never knew you." This is His judgment for those who have committed lawlessness.

> "This spirit of lawlessness is the same spirit that Satan used to deceive Eve when he told her, in so many words, 'God won't punish you for disobeying. You can eat the fruit and you won't have to pay for it!'" (www.worldchallenge.org)

Satan is using the same lie on *Christians* today; day after day, he convinces masses of *believers* that they can sin without paying any penalty. It is a demonic scheme to pervert Christ's gospel of peace. Tragically, many *lukewarm* Christians are succumbing to this spirit of lawlessness.

Paul says the Antichrist will rise to power because people will be blinded and deceived by their own sin. (See 2 Thessalonians 2:9-10.)

Notice that this excerpt refers to "lukewarm Christians." That seems to be an oxymoron. Christians who are lukewarm have what we call "one foot in the church and the other foot in the world." God is not pleased with that and states very harshly in the book of Revelation 3:15–17, "I know your works, that you are neither cold nor hot. So then, because you are lukewarm, and neither cold nor hot, I will vomit you out of my mouth."

This leads to the question, Why would God use a person to cast out demons or to prophesy or do great wonders if they are still sinning? Well, it's actually pretty simple. Because God's heart is for the souls of people, if need be, He will "use a donkey" (2 Peter 2:16; Numbers 22) to get His message to them. Whom or what He uses is of no matter. The bottom line is that His message reaches the hearts of people who need it. There are churches where the pastors are living ungodly lives, yet they still come before their congregations with powerful, God-ordained messages of hope, love, peace, and salvation. And people are getting saved under their leadership. Where does that leave that pastor or leader? Will God say to him or her, "Depart from me, I never knew you"?

They are saved, are they not? Again, there are many

who have honestly and sincerely received salvation. They really are saved. But I would be hard pressed to have to believe that someone whose life has not reflected any kind of relationship with the Lord apart from sitting in church on Sundays or the offering of an occasional, "God is good," will make it into heaven. I reflect upon the many times I could have died in my sins. To face God in that predicament, I wouldn't have made it in.

Of course, now, there is always forgiveness. But even with that, God says He looks at our hearts. Some use the "forgiveness card" as a right to continue to sin, assuming that all they have to do is say they're sorry and God will forgive them.

God knows the difference between those who are truly sorrowful and those whose hearts are far from it. Tomorrow is never promised. I would *not* chance my soul being eternally lost in hell because I don't want to live fully for God. Either you're saved or you're not, but you must understand that you're also either living for God or you're not. Lukewarm, as we have learned, is a nasty word to God.

In Matthew 15, beginning with verse 14, we learn of a man who, before leaving for his travels, calls "his servants" and gives them all one or more talents. There are some specific returns that the master expects from them based upon how the servants invest the talents.

When he returns and questions each one, they receive

either a reward or punishment based upon what the master finds. Verse 14 says, "For the kingdom of heaven is as a man travelling into a far country, who called his own servants, and delivered unto them his goods." Notice that this verse clearly refers to them as "his own servants." There was no distinction that differentiated some as servants and others as friends, or co-workers, visitors or beggars or any other outsider. They were "his own servants." They belonged to the master. Are you getting the point?

When the master returns and finds that one of "his servants" has not followed the same rule as was expected of the others, the master referred to him in verse 26 as, "you wicked and lazy servant." As a result, according to verse 30, the master declared, "cast the unprofitable 'servant' into the outer darkness. There will be weeping and gnashing of teeth."

Understand this: The "talent" for us who are saved (God's servants) is the gift of salvation by the crucifixion of His Son, Jesus. He gave us salvation (the talent) and expects, as a return on that gift, the investment of our very lives. When Jesus returns, He is going to want to know what we have done with His gift (talent). When we accepted Jesus as Savior, we accepted the talent from God. After accepting the talent, we must invest it in something that will bring a return. Thus, we begin to learn of God and how to live for him through the teaching of His Word. The purpose is so that we will be able to give positive accounts of what we (His servants) did with His talent (gift of salvation).

So, based upon what Jesus finds upon His return, we (His servants) will be separated, according to verse 34, which says, "Then shall the King say unto them on his right hand, Come, ye blessed of my Father, inherit the kingdom prepared for you from the foundation of the world." Verse 41 says, "Then shall he say also unto them on the left hand, Depart from me, ye cursed, into everlasting fire, prepared for the devil and his angels."

The analogy clearly refers to those who are saved and have supposedly made Jesus the Lord of their lives. God has specific expectations of us as His children, His servants. We are going to be held accountable to Him for what we did with His talents. Those on his left hand are not unsaved people. They are children of God who will have wasted God's talent, His gift of salvation, and will be eternally lost because they would have fallen for the lies of lawlessness.

Once saved, always saved? Yes! All saved people go to heaven? Think about it.

Hebrews 6:4 says, "For it is impossible for those who were once enlightened, and have tasted of the heavenly gift, and were made partakers of the Holy Ghost, And have tasted the good word of God, and the powers of the world to come, If they shall fall away, to renew them again unto repentance; seeing they crucify to themselves the Son of God afresh, and put him to an open shame."

Jesus died for us. We're in or we're out. Jesus is not going to die for us all over again just because some accepted His salvation and at some point, fell away never again aligning their lives with God's expectations of us as *His servants.*

We must decide if we are going to fully live out our salvation for God or not at all. There is no in between. There is no straddling the fence. There is no "it doesn't take all that," because it does take all that.

1 Chronicles 21:24 teaches us about King David being offered gifts but refusing them, saying, "I will not take something that costs me nothing."

Jesus died on the cross—our sins cost Him His life. We should expect to give Him no less. In Acts 21, the apostle Paul was warned not to go to Jerusalem because there were Jews who were waiting to bind him and deliver him to the Gentiles. His traveling companions pleaded with him not to go.

But Paul, with holy indignation, responded, "I'm not only ready to be bound but also to die for the name of the Lord." He also professed in 2 Corinthians 12:10, "Therefore I take pleasure in infirmities, in reproaches, in needs, persecutions, in distresses, for Christ's sake."

Yes, it does take all that. It is the exchange we make for the talent, God's gift of salvation; it is the return on

His investment that He will expect when He returns for us.

Many of the people sitting in your churches, so-named Christians, don't realize this. How many of your saved church members have come to that place of "all to Jesus I surrender"? Think about it. If we can live any kind of way and still make it in, what is the purpose of giving our all to the cause of Christ if those who live any way they want and do whatever they want can get into heaven just as easily as those who walk the straight and narrow?

> "For the time has come for judgment to begin at the house of God; and if it begins with us first, what will be the end of those who do not obey the gospel of God? Now If the righteous one is scarcely saved, Where will the ungodly and the sinner appear?" (1 Peter 4:17–18 NKJV)

It must be impressed upon the hearts and minds of those who profess to be Christian, the seriousness of "without spot or wrinkle." Are we perfect? Not at all. Will we make mistakes? Will we sin? Yes, of course. As long as we are in this fallible state, we are apt to fall. But does that excuse us? No.

There is a reason the prayer in Matthew 6 says, "forgive us … as we forgive." If we sincerely love God and want to be in right standing with Him, He will forgive a heart that is truly longing to please Him. In Psalm 51, King David offers the perfect example of a penitent heart. After all the egregious sin he'd committed, God still said that David was a man after His own heart. Why? because David's heart was grievous, in a true state of sorrow. It devastated David to know that he had broken God's heart … he had sinned against God. God saw David's heart, which is why He spoke such an accolade over David. In spite of everything David had done, the deepest longing of his heart was to please. We should follow his example.

Where is the Church?

Years ago, a friend told me that he believed the Bible when it said that people would be judged someday. He added, however, that he didn't see the need to make any attempts to actually follow what it said because, in his interpretation, "It's all prearranged." He accepted that some people would go to hell and some to heaven. But because of his opinion that everything in the Bible is prearranged, there was nothing anyone could do about that predestined end (you'd be surprised by what people believe).

I was desperate in my need to undo that misinterpretation, so I tried again and again to explain it to him. John 13:11 says, "For He knew who would betray Him; therefore, He said, 'You are not all clean.'"

It says in John 6:64, "But there are some of you that believe not. For Jesus knew from the beginning who they were that believed not, and who should betray him." In John 6:70: "Jesus answered them, Have not I chosen you twelve, and one of you is a devil?" Though He chose twelve disciples, Jesus already knew that Judas would betray Him. Isaiah 43:13 God says, "Yea, before the day was I am He." He is before all things.

So it is with us. It is not that things are prearranged, as my friend believed. But because He's God, He already knows who will accept Him and who will reject Him. He has given us all a free will and allows us to choose. He already knows those who were moved only by a momentary fear of hell and were merely choosing fire insurance. He also already knows of those who will pursue Him and His will love Him with *all* their hearts, minds, souls, and strength. He won't send anyone to hell; it will have been a choice.

Where is the Church?

Are you preparing your members? Are you teaching them the proper and true way to relationship with God? Are you?

Jeremiah 23:1–2 says, "'Woe to the shepherds who destroy and scatter the sheep of My pasture!' says the Lord. Therefore, thus says the Lord God of Israel against the shepherds who feed my people: 'You have scattered my flock, driven them away, and not attended to them.

Behold I will attend to you for the evil of your doings,' says the Lord."

Shepherds, church leaders, you must admonish your people by telling them that they are required to be more than just faithful church members. Inquire as to whether they might need to rethink things, for they must be ready to meet God in peace. You *who have rule over* the people to whom God has assigned to you, must "watch for their souls, as those who must give account. Pray, pastors, church leaders, that you can do so with joy and not with grief, for that would be unprofitable for you" (Hebrews 13:17).

Chapter 9
An Evangelist's Heart

At age twelve or thirteen, my sisters and I were playing across the street from our house where we lived with our grandmother. My grandmother's house was across from the stadium where the Atlanta Braves played. The big parking lot separated her house from the stadium. One day, while sitting on the gravel of that parking lot, a man and his wife suddenly towered over us. He introduced himself and his wife and said he was going to be the pastor of a church and was renovating a house that just happened to be only two or three doors down from my grandmother's house. He was extending an invitation for us to visit.

We thought the man was crazy. He was telling us about this God who loved us, telling us to come to visit his church so we could learn about Jesus, etc. Though we had gone to church occasionally as small children, we had never been made to understand anything about God or Jesus in the relationship sense of the word. So we just said okay and let them move along.

Believe it or not, nearly every week for almost a year we'd look up and this same man, this pastor, was back again, asking us to come visit his church. He was going from door to door up and down our street and throughout the neighborhood, doing the same, inviting people to visit his church. When we saw him coming, we'd yell, "Here comes that preacher," and run and hide in a big closet, hoping he would just go away if we ignored his knocks.

But my grandmother was so accustomed to his appearances that she would open the door and let him in. We absolutely hated that because he would come in and stay and talk to my grandmother for what seemed like hours while we were stuck in that closet.

After a while, one of my sisters decided to go to his church. One Sunday, after visiting his church for literally the first time, she came home and made a beeline to her clothes in the closet and dresser drawers. She pulled out all her pants and started to unthread the legs for the purpose of making them into skirts.

We were dumbfounded by her odd behavior. "What's wrong with you?" we asked.

She said, "I'm saved now, and as a Christian, I can no longer wear pants."

We were like, "You're what now? You're a what?"

It made absolutely no sense. She was also getting rid of jewelry and said she could no longer dance and do other stuff that was of the devil.

"Of the what?" We were totally stupefied! We didn't know what to make of it and thought she had been bewitched or brainwashed.

But she was adamant and unchanging, and from that day at the age of about eleven or twelve, until she left for college, she was devoted to her newfound beliefs.

Slowly but surely her unwavering faith began to tug at us. At some point, each of us went to her church. At first it was honestly out of curiosity, just to see what this craziness was that our sister had gotten herself caught up in.

I was the last one to go. When I finally decided to go, it was because I was just tired of being the only one left at home without my sisters.

I remember my first visit and how the pastor taught about God. I remember how he used the Bible to explain the whole story of salvation through Jesus. I can still feel my heart swell as I listened intently to this great love that God had for us. I am still winded when I remember how he expounded so intently on the severe punishment that Jesus took for us. I was so moved. I cried and cried. I felt as if my heart would burst.

Then, the pivotal moment came when the pastor invited, to the front of the church, those who wanted to be saved. He said he would pray with us and help us receive Jesus. I felt suddenly paralyzed with fear and intimidation. I wanted to go, but I was so afraid to go before the church.

But he said, "If you don't want to come up, that's okay; just know that God will hear you wherever you are."

I listened carefully and held on to the words that he recited as the prayer of salvation. When I got home, I went into our bedroom, got down on my knees at the edge of the bed, and prayed that exact prayer to God. It is as real today as it was those more than forty-five years ago. That is how I know it's real. That is how I know Jesus saved me. When I stood up, I sensed in my heart that Jesus was now my Savior.

I told my new pastor that I had prayed the prayer of salvation. He said that now that I was a Christian, the next step was to read the Bible and pray. That was all the explanation I got.

I said, "okay," and began my trek toward knowing this God that I had received. It was all done out of obedience and a desire to grow in my newfound faith. Little did I know that all these years later, that obedient reading of the Word of God would make me very learned in scripture, and that obedience to constant prayer would make me an intercessor and prayer warrior. So although I didn't get an official explanation, and though I didn't really understand all the hows or whys, it really did work out for my good.

I felt a longing in my heart to share Jesus with others. Our pastor's wife would take us through "soul winning" classes and practice sessions. We would role play different scenarios of people we might meet, and then we hit the streets. My pastor made it very clear that we had been called to share our faith. So, again, out of obedience, I was telling everybody.

I remember being fourteen or fifteen years old and hearing my mom telling people who would ask, "What is she doing?" "Oh, she does that all the time," my mom would respond."

Years later, I look back and realize that where I've worked or lived, there are very few people that I have not told about salvation through Jesus Christ. I found that it was no longer an obedient act. It had become an obsession, a weighty desire in my heart to see people saved.

I still felt, however, that I was simply doing what we were expected to do as Christians. I remember telling my oldest sister once, "It's no big deal. It's what we're supposed to do, right? Don't all Christians tell people about Jesus?"

She said, "Oh no, not the way you do it." Of course, I didn't know what she meant.

More years passed, and the pastor of the church we belonged to in Miami told me that God had called me to evangelize. At that time, being in the Baptist church, we were not taught about the fivefold offices, and I had no idea what he meant. Yes, I was always telling people about Jesus, but I didn't know there was a name for what I was doing.

"The steps of a good man are ordered by the Lord," the Bible says. And as God would have it, we eventually ended up in a prophetic church where the apostolic and prophetic ministries were being taught. That is when I learned of the fivefold offices and when the office of the evangelist was prophesied to me.

In the times that we live in now, I have to be very careful not to allow my heart for the lost to overwhelm me. Sometimes my heart hurts so badly for those who don't know the Lord that I feel literal pain in my chest. Tears come to my eyes, and I feel weighted down by the truth that many are not going to make it to eternal life in Jesus … that many are going to hell.

It was prophesied to me years ago that God said I carry a longing to see souls saved the way He does. That was overwhelming to me, but I understood it clearly. I've often asked Him, like Paul asked him to remove his thorn in the flesh, to take the heaviness of it from my heart. But I have also had to hear God say to me like He said to Paul, "No, I will not remove it because my grace is sufficient for you."

Transparent moment: I honestly have found myself saying to God, "I wish I were never born. It hurts too much to have to accept that there are more that are lost than are saved or even going to be." I have found myself saying, "I don't like teetering on the edge of fear for my own son's salvation." But God! He promised me that all my family will be saved so I have had to be like Abraham and, "not waver at the promises of God." I try to be happy when a child is born, but deep in my heart, I'm saying, "Oh, here's another life that will eventually have to decide the destiny of his or her soul." Crazy, huh? God has to constantly calm me down and tell me to stay in my lane. He is God … not me. I'm to carry the souls, yes, but I'm not to become overwhelmed by them.

I realize that if God relieves me of this deep longing to see the lost saved, I'm afraid I won't want to go after them the way that I do. I have had to allow the Lord to give me balance. I have had to allow God to remind me that He is God and this burden is His to carry, not mine. I'm only to be his heart extended to those who will receive it.

Sadly, from the time I was thirteen years old until this very day, I've watched the depravity of the human race. I've watched and witnessed the wicked schemes and deceptions of Satan consume the souls of people so much so that they are blind and deaf to the truth that Jesus was and is and will always be the *only* way to God. The assignment of the evangelists and all those who know the Lord is to intercede for the souls of people so they can be set free, to pray for their feet to be snatched from the bondage of the net of hell, that their eyes and ears will be opened to see and hear and accept the truth of the gospel of Jesus Christ. There is so much resistance to truth.

Though many have come against it, Christianity will never go away. But in an effort to cloud and muddy God's Word, mixture from opposing religions and beliefs have left many wondering, *What is the real truth?* It's as if the opposers have concluded, "If we can't beat them, let's join them. Just make sure that they still don't get to this Jesus."

Many people have become like dead men walking. They are alive and breathing and functioning but are clueless to the fact that they are on the path that leads to everlasting destruction.

My one heart's desire is like that of our Savior, Jesus, that all people everywhere would be saved. While we are supposed to pursue life in every arena, while we are to pursue success and wholeness and wellness, the bottom line remains, "What does it profit us to gain the world and end up losing our souls?"

What will it have been worth? We've got it backward. Everything we are and everything we're supposed to do and everything we're supposed to be stems from initially knowing Jesus as Savior, Lord, and the One who has the plans for our lives already laid out. We know His Word says, "Those plans are good." The world has gotten so caught up in the hustle and bustle of the rat race that a relationship with God is displaced or never pursued at all.

When we stand before God, power, position, and possessions will matter not. He will want to know, "What did you do with my talent? What did you do with my Son's death on the cross for you? Did you honor my Son's sacrifice for you?"

What are *you* going to do differently to make sure people under your watch are prepared? God still commands us to "Go" and "Compel."

Where's the church?

Let's *go*!

> "Behold, I am coming quickly! Blessed is he who keeps the words of the prophecy of this book" (Revelation 22:7 NKJV).

Chapter 10
Decision Time

Perhaps reading this book has caused you to reflect, to seriously contemplate the condition of your own life, your own destiny. Perhaps you thought you were in God's will and ready to meet the Lord in peace. Perhaps you realized there are people under your care who are also not truly in right standing with the Lord.

The Lord is not willing for *any* to perish but that *all* would come to repentance. As long as there is breath in your body, there is time to come into right relationship with the Lord, whether you are saved or unsaved.

Take this time to talk to the Lord. He's with you now and ready to hear your heart of repentance. It's not too late to get it right. He suffers long with us and is gracious and full of mercy. He is listening. Do it now. Tomorrow is not promised.

Though there is much strife and suffering and

affliction in this world, it really is God's will that we live His abundant life which, of course, is only found in Him.

You may reach me at janiney1107@yahoo.com, on my Facebook page, or write to me at The Fusion Centre, 16400 NW 15th Avenue, Miami Gardens, FL 33169.

Afterword

If, after reading this profound and thought-provoking book, you realize that you have never accepted Jesus Christ into your life as Savior and Lord, now is the time. Tomorrow is never promised. The Word of God tells us in II Corinthians 5:10 that "we must all stand before the judgment seat of Christ." It also tells us in Hebrews 9:27 that "it is appointed unto us 'once' to die, but after this the judgment."

We are all Words spoken from heaven by God Himself. We are all placed into the earth with a God-ordained purpose. What a sad state of affairs it would be to have lived and died, never having accomplished that purpose, or worse yet, to face God without ever having accepted His *free* gift of salvation.

For a heart-convicting and convincing view of a life that has accepted the Lord versus a life apart from a relationship with God, view the YouTube video: "Where do we go when we die?" at https://youtu.be/GhKUU4waDTI.

If you want to accept the Lord into your heart and life as your Savior, pray this simple prayer. If you mean it from your heart, the spirit of the Lord will come in, solidifying your place in the family of God:

"Dear God, I realize that I am a sinner in need of your salvation. I know now that Jesus died on the cross and rose again for the sole purpose of providing the way for me to be back in right relationship with You. I ask You to forgive me for all my sins. I ask Jesus to come into my heart. I receive Jesus as my Savior, and I make Him the Lord of my life. Thank You, Lord, for saving me. In Jesus's name, amen!"

Praying that simple but heartfelt prayer is your guarantee of eternal life in God. *Welcome to the family of God!*

If you need further direction about how to get started in your new relationship with God, email me at janiney1107@yahoo.com.

About the Author

Janine Y. Ross was saved at the age of thirteen. Though it took her quite a number of years to fully walk in the call God had on her life, looking back she realized that from a young age, God called her as an Evangelist. Her heart carries the heartbeat of God for lost souls.

She is a middle school reading teacher in Broward County, Florida, and is the proud mother of one son, Deon Ross, who is a personal fitness trainer.

Additionally, she professes that one of the best things that happened in her life was to meet and become under the leadership and tutelage of Dr. Ursula T. Wright, CEO and founder of The Fusion Centre in Miami Gardens, Florida. She credits Dr. Wright for being her scaffold and for bringing clarity and stability to her life in God.

This, her second book, is heavy with the burden of God's heart for those who are unsaved. You may find her first writing, *Kingdom Insights, Encouragement When You Need Answers,* on Amazon.com.

Bibliography

Abington School District v. Schempp—Wikipedia. https://en.wikipedia.org/wiki/Abington_School_ District_v._Schempp.

Animal Myths Busted—National Geographic Kids: why It's Not True: Ostriches don't bury their heads in the sand. https://kids.nationalgeographic.com/explore/ nature/animal-myths-busted/.

Carlton Pearson—Wikipedia, The Gospel of Inclusion. https://en.wikipedia.org/wiki/Carlton_Pearson,

Reverend Ike—Wikipedia, Life and Career. https://en.wikipedia.org/wiki/Reverend_Ike.

Universal reconciliation—Wikipedia https://en.wikipedia. org/wiki/Universal_reconciliation.

Printed in the United States
By Bookmasters